Stopping the Self-Sabotage

Healthy Mindsets for Success

Table of Contents

Chapter 1. Introduction

Welcome to a comprehensive journey into the realm of potential, productivity, and personal success: "Stopping the Self-Sabotage: Healthy Mindsets for Success". This special report is tailored specifically to dive deep into one of the most significant challenges individuals face when aiming for success - self-sabotage. Delivered with love and backed by psychological findings, this uplifting guide is set to empower you, provide you with strategies to overcome internal hindrances and fortify a mindset paving the way to success. Ready for a spectacular transformation? Let's embark on this journey together and start constructing a life you've always dreamt of! Don't just dream, action it – and this masterfully crafted report is your first step towards that. Get excited because your best self is just around the corner!

Chapter 2. Understanding the Phenomenon of Self-Sabotage

Self-sabotage can be defined as the process where we create obstacles and excuses that prevent us from taking action towards what we want most in life. It often stems from unconscious thoughts and behaviors that undermine our self-worth, making us feel undeserving of success.

2.1. Recognizing Common Forms of Self-Sabotage

Among the many forms self-sabotage can take, procrastination is perhaps the most common. This typically happens when we delay or avoid tasks, often out of fear of failure or discomfort. We might tell ourselves that we're waiting for the perfect time or the right mood to get started, but the reality is, the perfect time often never comes, and this becomes an excuse for inaction.

Another common mode of self-sabotage is perfectionism, which is an all-or-nothing mindset where anything less than perfect is a failure. This is a destructive thought pattern that puts incredible pressure on us and can deter us from even trying.

Moreover, some people sabotage themselves emotionally by engaging in negative self-talk or pessimistic thinking. These individuals often hold a negative image of themselves which they reinforce with their words, actions, and thoughts.

Lastly, comfort-seeking is another form of self-sabotage where individuals choose safety, familiarity and immediate gratification over the longer-term benefits that comes with enduring discomfort for personal growth. They might overindulge in comfort foods, binge-watch TV, or excessively use social media to distract themselves from their goals or responsibilities.

2.2. Understanding the Root Causes

Many psychologists believe that self-sabotage is an offshoot of low self-esteem and fear.

Self-esteem refers to the overall opinion we have of ourselves, which is usually established during early childhood and solidified during adolescence. Experiences that lead to feelings of rejection, criticism or failure can easily instill a deep-seated sense of inadequacy and unworthiness - the pivot point for sabotaging behaviors.

Fear, on the other hand, plays a pivotal role in self-sabotage as the fear of failure, success, and even change can terrify people into inaction. Fear of failure arises when you're scared of making mistakes or not living up to expectations. Fear of success relates to an underlying worry that achieving one's goals might lead to an excess of responsibilities or standards to uphold. Fear of change is tied to the fear of uncertainty and the unknown. Any measure of success in life invariably implies some extent of change, and this can spark fear and in turn, self-sabotage.

2.3. Impact on Your Life

The sabotage cycle can have severe implications on one's mental, emotional, and even physical well-being.

From the mental perspective, it prevents personal growth and learning. It can result in chronic demotivation and dissatisfaction with life, leading to conditions such as depression, anxiety, and stress.

The emotional impact of self-sabotage can manifest as feelings of guilt, helplessness, and regret. These feelings can destroy our self-esteem and confidence, creating barriers to happiness and satisfaction.

Physically, repeated acts of self-sabotage can affect our health. Chronic stress and anxiety, often stemming from persistent self-sabotage, can have adverse effects on the body, leading to conditions such as hypertension, heart diseases, and obesity.

Bluntly put, self-sabotage is a major roadblock on your path to success and can prevent you from reaching your full potential, both personally and professionally.

2.4. Stepping into Self-Awareness

The journey to overcoming self-sabotage begins with self-awareness. We need to develop an understanding and clarity about our thoughts, feelings, and behaviors, as our internal reality dictates our external reality.

Awareness brings to light the patterns, narratives, and scripts that we unconsciously follow in our lives. Only by bringing these patterns into our conscious awareness are we able to challenge and change them.

By embracing tools like journaling, mindfulness, meditation, and therapy, we can begin to uncover and understand the mechanisms of our self-sabotage. Doing this work is a courageous act, but remember, no significant changes come without discomfort.

Overcoming self-sabotage isn't about becoming a different person but about challenging your self-destructive thoughts and behaviors and fostering those which propel you towards success. It surely isn't an easy journey, but one that holds the power to transform your life for the better.

Remember, when you stop sabotaging yourself, you begin to become the person you've always dreamed of being. So, start today and step into a brighter, more fulfilling future tomorrow.

Chapter 3. The Psychological Triggers of Self-Sabotage

Self-sabotage is a complex psychological pattern rooted in various triggers and dynamics. To understand how self-sabotage unravels, it is essential first to grasp the psychological triggers which propel these destructive patterns.

3.1. The Intricacies of Fear

Fear acts as a critical catalyst propelling self-sabotage. From a psychological angle, fear can manifest in various forms, with some common ones being fear of failure, fear of success, fear of uncertainty, and fear of judgment.

Fear of failure is often sourced from past disappointments or instilled beliefs forming an obstacle in taking action towards goals. On the flip side, fear of success emanates from the scare of being unable to handle the possible responsibilities, public scrutiny, and expectations following triumph.

Fear of uncertainty and fear of judgment function similarly, creating apprehension towards exploring unfamiliar choices or taking steps that might induce criticism.

3.2. The Self-Concept Dilemma

Another factor triggering self-sabotage is the perceived self-concept, i.e., the individual's belief about who they are and what they can achieve. Formed from personal experiences, societal influences, and upbringing, this concept can either act as the wind beneath the wings or the weight pulling down aspirations. In its negative form, limited self-belief leads to the manifestation of self-sabotage.

Some might perceive themselves unworthy of success due to a distorted self-concept, leading them to subconsciously derail their progress towards achieving goals. In contrast, others might believe they lack the necessary skills required for accomplishment, triggering a sense of defeat even before beginning their journey.

3.3. Two-Faced Perfectionism

Perfectionism, while traditionally viewed positively, has a dark side that triggers self-sabotage. There exists a distinction between adaptive perfectionists, who harbor high standards and display resilience while aiming for their goals, and maladaptive perfectionists, who associate their self-worth with the impeccable execution of tasks.

Maladaptive perfectionism often leads to procrastination, owing to the fear of producing less than ideal results. This fear can lead to a destructive loop of delaying tasks and eventually self-sabotaging.

3.4. Past Conditioning and Experiences

Past experiences, especially those from childhood, play a vital role in shaping future behaviors. If an individual faced severe criticism, lack of validation, or trauma in the past, they might establish damaging patterns repeating in future scenarios.

For example, a person who faced frequent criticism during childhood might internalize the belief that they can never do "good enough." This belief may later create situations of self-sabotage in both their personal and professional life.

Similarly, individuals with past trauma might create a protective shell around themselves to avoid experiencing vulnerability or pain again. This protection can morph into resistance against trying new things, exploring potential opportunities, or making an effort towards achieving personal or professional growth – all signs of self-sabotage.

3.5. The Ebb and Flow of Emotional Regulation

Poor emotional regulation also acts as a trigger for self-sabotage. Those who struggle to identify, understand and manage their emotions may resort to self-sabotaging behaviors as a form of escape, distraction, or self-punishment.

For instance, an individual dealing with job stress might resort to overeating, substance abuse, or inconsistent sleep patterns, all of which can derail their overall health and job performance.

3.6. Negative Mindset and Habitual Patterns

Finally, long-ingrained negative habitual patterns also contribute to the cycle of self-sabotage. These patterns could include a habitual negative mindset, constant self-depreciative talk, or negative behavioral patterns such as procrastination and avoidance.

These triggers work in tandem, reinforcing the sabotage and making it increasingly difficult to break through the cycle. Thus, understanding them is the first step towards breaking free.

In the next chapters, we will delve into methods to overcome these triggers, replacing them with healthier thought patterns and behaviors. Insight, awareness, and deliberate practice can help break the pattern of self-sabotage, promoting an empowering and successful life narrative.

Chapter 4. Unmasking the Subconscious: Hidden Intentions Behind Self-doubt

Human sentiment is a complex web, forever intertwining and often tangled beyond our immediate understanding. It's further compounded by an elusive character playing puppeteer to our emotions, decisions, and actions: the subconscious. One of its key agents that affect our journey towards success is self-doubt. Dark and nebulous, it whispers tales of uncertainty and potential failure in our ears, often obstructing us from chasing our dreams. To tackle this unwelcome visitor, we first need to unmask it, comprehend its origins, and deconstruct its intentions.

4.1. The Metaphorical Iceberg: Conscious vs. Subconscious Mind

A prevalent metaphor to illustrate the workings of the human mind uses an iceberg. The tip signifies our conscious mind, comprising thoughts and emotions we are aware of. Below water, the massive body symbolizes our subconscious, functioning out of our conscious perception. Key psychological theories suggest that our subconscious often guides our behaviour more than our consciously made decisions, creating tremendous implications on our life paths and success metrics.

The subconscious mind is the storage house of countless memories, experiences, values, and beliefs, forming our unique personal schema. This schema not only shapes our perception of the world but also interacts with our conscious thought processes. Notably, it plays a commanding role in the inception and fueling of self-doubt.

4.2. A Genesis in the Shadows: The Birthplace of Self-Doubt

From a psychological standpoint, self-doubt is a multi-faceted concept. It can stem from past experiences, societal expectations, or a nagging fear of failure or rejection—each sourced and nurtured in the depths of our subconscious mind. We can trace it back to negative feedback received in childhood, subconscious assimilation of devaluating societal norms, or even an instinctual, subconscious desire to avoid threat and harm.

Childhood experiences notably play a pivotal role. From parental admonishments to peers' ridicule or even a teacher's casual remark, these experiences could seed self-doubt in a child's impressionable mind. Imbued deep within the subconscious layers, this potent source for self-doubt can linger throughout adulthood, eroding confidence and corroding potential for success.

4.3. Society's Mirroring Maze: Expectations, Comparisons, and Inadequacy

The society we grow in is like a giant mirroring maze where we continuously compare, evaluate, and judge ourselves against others. This societal mirror reflects not just our perceived inadequacies but also subconsciously implanted definitions of success.

Subconsciously, our minds are often so engrossed in these reflections that we start accepting societal portrayals as our reality. These deep-rooted beliefs can ignite a chronic sense of self-doubt, deterring us from realizing our full potential and defining our success.

4.4. A Tug-of-war in Shadow: Limiting Beliefs and Self-Sabotage

A significant by-product of this subconscious interplay is the creation of limiting beliefs. These are subconscious assumptions about our capabilities and potential that become mental shackles, barricading our road to success.

A sinister consequence of such beliefs is self-sabotage—where we inadvertently hinder our progress or potential success. Rooted in self-doubt, this behaviour is a subconscious defense mechanism to protect ourselves from anticipated failure or rejection.

4.5. Illuminating the Shadows: Unveiling Hidden Intentions

As we peer deeper into the shadow of our subconscious intentions, a paradox emerges. The subconscious mind, designed to protect us, can end up becoming our adversary. Self-doubt, instead of being a protective armour, can stifle growth and inhibit success.

Our task then is not to banish this shadow but to illuminate it with understanding. Discerning self-doubt's causes and intentions, we can then decouple it from our idea of self, disempowering its relentless grip on our minds and actions.

Unmasking occurs in acknowledging self-doubt as a creation of our subconscious mind, drawing upon past experiences and societal constructs. It paves the way for understanding that this entity isn't us but rather a part of the schema we have adopted.

4.6. The Counterintuitive Key: Embracing Self-doubt

The initial key to dealing with self-doubt is counterintuitive: embracing it. There is a profound strength in acceptance — it provides clarity, promotes understanding, and opens doors for transformation.

By recognising self-doubt as a subconscious construct, we simultaneously give ourselves the power to challenge and change it. Rather than a destroyer of dreams, we start viewing self-doubt as a catalyst for introspection and growth.

It is our role, then, to recognize the silent workings of our subconscious, bring it into the sphere of conscious dialogue, and harness it for our growth. In the following chapters, we'll dive deeper into techniques to overpower self-doubt, reshape limiting beliefs, and dismantle the barriers to success. The thereby illuminated subconscious will become an ally in our journey towards personal success, the journey that we are all destined to embark on.

Chapter 5. Overcoming Procrastination: The Silent Self-Saboteur

Successful development and achievement of goals often run into an unseen but familiar obstacle: Procrastination. We are all guilty of it at one point or another, delaying or postponing tasks deemed necessary or important, to a later time. Psychologists postulate that this tendency originates from an inner battle between our present and future selves, where the present self is typically the victor, thanks to its immediate demands and impulses. Let's delve into this pertinent issue constraining productivity, examine the anatomy of procrastination, understand why we do it, and more importantly, look at strategies to defeat this silent enemy within.

5.1. Understanding Procrastination

At its core, procrastination is the act of delaying or postponing tasks or actions. It's the gap between intention and action, between the planning and the doing. The term was coined from the Latin 'pro,' meaning forward, and 'crastinus,' meaning of tomorrow. Thus, a procrastinator is essentially someone who forwards tasks to tomorrow.

Procrastination isn't a sign of laziness. Often, it speaks more about our emotional state and how we deal with stress, pressure, task aversion, fear of failure, or lack of confidence. Unfortunately, it can become an unhealthy cycle that not only negatively impacts productivity but also mental health.

5.2. The Costs of Procrastination

Procrastination, as harmless as it may seem, carries substantial costs. These costs can be summed up as productivity losses, unfulfilled potential, health implications like stress and, in a larger picture, can lead to missed opportunities and regret. On a more immediate level, procrastination disrupts our schedules and creates a knock-on effect, affecting subsequent tasks and, ultimately, our personal and professional objectives.

5.3. The Habit Loop: Cue, Routine, and Reward

According to Charles Duhigg in his book, 'The Power of Habit', every habit consists of a cue (the trigger of the habit), routine (the act itself), and reward (the gratification from performing the habit). Procrastination is no exception. Recognizing and understanding your habit loop of procrastination is key to overcoming it.

For instance, your procrastination habit loop could be:

1. Cue: Feeling overwhelmed by a large task.

2. Routine: Deciding to do it 'later' and instead indulging in low-effort activities.

3. Reward: Short-term relief of stress.

By identifying your habit loop, you can develop a strategy to counter it.

5.4. Six Strategies to Overcome Procrastination

1. Breaking Tasks Down: The 'kid sister' of procrastination is

overwhelm. We often procrastinate because we feel the task at hand is too large or intimidating. Therefore, breaking down a significant task into smaller, manageable chunks helps reduce the feeling of overwhelm, enabling us to make a start and maintain momentum.

2. Time Blocking: This technique involves setting aside specific chunks of time to tackle the task we're avoiding. During these periods, all other distractions are eliminated, ensuring undivided attention.

3. Use the Power of Sufficiency: Aim for 'sufficient' and not 'perfect.' Striving for perfection often leads to stalling. Instead, target sufficiency, the feeling of "enough for now," which helps us move forward.

4. The Pomodoro Technique: This time management tactic involves working in focused 25-minute intervals, separated by 5-minutes breaks. Every fourth break is longer, typically around 15-30 minutes. These parameters can be adjusted according to comfort.

5. Use Eisenhower Matrix: Named after President Dwight D. Eisenhower, this matrix categorizes tasks in four quadrants as per their urgency and importance. It helps in aligning our activities with their significance and urgency, allowing better use of time and effort.

6. Conquering Fear: A deep-seated fear of failure often fuels procrastination. Challenging these fears and understanding that failure is part of the process, not a detriment to it, can help navigate this obstacle.

5.5. Using Technology to Your Advantage

Several apps and tools are designed to tackle procrastination. Tools like Trello and Todoist are fantastic for managing tasks, while

RescueTime and Forest can help maintain focus.

Moreover, virtual personal assistants like Alexa or Google Assistant can also be used to set reminders, deadlines, and manage to-do lists effectively.

5.6. Conclusion: The Journey to Overcoming Procrastination

Overcoming procrastination is a journey that requires deliberate effort and practice. An understanding of why we procrastinate, along with strategies to resist it, can play a massive role in combating this issue. It's important to remember that you are more powerful than your strongest excuse. As Mark Twain once said, "The secret of getting ahead is getting started."

By empowering ourselves with the right tools and mindset to conquer procrastination, we not only enhance our productivity but also take a crucial step towards unshackling ourselves from the chains of self-sabotage and inching closer to our visions of success. Remember, every journey starts with a single step. Don't wait for tomorrow, start today!

Chapter 6. Developing a Success-Oriented Mindset: The Role of Positive Affirmations

The first and perhaps most vital step along the road to personal success lies in the construction and cultivation of a success-oriented mindset. This mental framework effectively serves as the foundation for all the goals you wish to achieve and the milestones you dream of reaching. Success, after all, is not a destination but an ongoing journey—one that requires an optimistic perspective and a growth mindset.

6.1. Understanding the Power of a Success-Oriented Mindset

A success-oriented mindset is one that perceives opportunities rather than obstacles, views failures as learning experiences instead of perceived setbacks, and constantly seeks room for improvement. It's the kind of mindset that doesn't settle for the status quo but fosters the conviction and resilience necessary for personal and professional advancement.

Why is such a mindset so crucial? Cognitive psychology theory can provide insights into the workings of our mind, more specifically how our thoughts, feelings, and beliefs can dictate our actions and behaviors. When you host a success-oriented mindset, you inevitably drive yourself towards success-inducing actions, eradicating self-defeating behaviors and encouraging constructive habits.

6.2. The Magic of Positive Affirmations

One of the most potent tools in instilling a success-oriented mindset is the use of positive affirmations. Positive affirmations are essentially uplifting statements that help you change your negative or unhelpful thoughts into positive, success-driving ones.

Here's how they work. Our brains are naturally predisposed to adopting patterns, including thought patterns. Repetitive negative thinking can instill a self-defeating mindset, whilst replacing these harmful thoughts with positive affirmations can shift our overall perspective and reprogram our thinking.

6.3. Crafting Your Personal Positive Affirmations

To derive the most significant benefits from positive affirmations, they must be personal, realistic, present-tensed, and positive. Here's a simple step-by-step guide to crafting your own powerful positive affirmations:

1. Identify negative thoughts or beliefs.

2. Challenge these beliefs.

3. Construct a positive affirmation that contradicts the negative thought.

4. Repeat your affirmations daily, preferably in front of a mirror.

An example of a positive affirmation may be: "I am worthy of success and happiness".

6.4. Evidential Power of Positive Affirmations: What Does Science Say?

Various psychological studies have backed the empowering effects of positive affirmations. Research published in the journal "Psychological Science" revealed that individuals who practiced self-affirmations demonstrated an increase in their problem-solving capacities under stress. Similarly, another study in the "Journal of Experimental Social Psychology" showed that affirmations could protect against the detrimental effects of stress on problem-solving performance.

6.5. Integrating Positive Affirmations into Your Daily Routine

Incorporating positive affirmations into your daily routine can drastically boost their effectiveness. They can be recited as a part of your morning routine, written down in a journal, or repeated mentally during meditations.

6.6. Dealing with Inevitable Setbacks: Maintaining a Success-Oriented Mindset

No journey towards success is void of challenges or setbacks. These are inevitable but what ultimately matters is how you perceive and react to them. Maintaining a success-oriented mindset despite the obstacles entails viewing setbacks as temporary and isolated events—opportunities disguised as challenges.

As you venture further into your personal success journey, remember that instilling a success-oriented mindset is ongoing work. It's a mental garden you must tend to every day, rooting out unhelpful thoughts and nurturing your positive affirmations. And in time, you'll see your personal growth mirror the blossoming of your mental garden, reflecting the spectacular transformation you've undergone on your road to success.

You hold the power to be the architect of your life. Embrace it, starting with your mindset—all the way to the manifestation of your goals and dreams. Remember, your best self is not a detour, but the result of a carefully paved road, which begins with developing a success-oriented mindset. This, paired with the potent practice of positive affirmations, is your essential toolkit for designing the expanse of your success. Time to get started, then! The journey of a thousand miles begins with a single step; let this inner transformation be yours.

Chapter 7. Resilience and Perseverance: Crucial Tools to Sidestep Self-sabotage

The essence of resilience and perseverance reveals in how we respond to challenges, setbacks, and failures. These are not just attributes but powerful tools in our life toolbox that can help squash self-sabotage. When wielded correctly, they foster a mentality of growth, fortitude, and progress.

7.1. Understanding Self-Sabotage

Before we delve into the heart of resilience and perseverance, it's salient to fully understand the beast we're trying to conquer: self-sabotage. Self-sabotage is when we actively or passively inhibit ourselves from reaching our goals. Subconscious fears or a sense of unworthiness often drive these actions. As a result, we might indulge in procrastination, self medicating with drugs or alcohol, overeating, or dwelling on negative thoughts.

7.2. Why Resilience and Perseverance?

In the pursuit of success, challenges are natural occurrences, but how we perceive and tackle them radically affects our journey's outcome. This is where resilience and perseverance come into play. They are the protective armor shielding us from the perils of self-sabotage, as they help us view challenges not as insurmountable obstacles but as opportunities for growth.

7.3. Building Resilience

Resilience is our ability to bounce back from setbacks. It's our psychological immune system that allows us to navigate through the ebbs and flows of life. Here are some steps to enhance your resilience:

1. Cultivate Positivity: Maintain an optimistic outlook. It's not about ignoring negative events but about interpreting and reacting to them healthily.

2. Embrace Change: Change is inevitable. Acknowledge its presence and adapt.

3. Invest in Relationships: Forge strong, supportive relationships. These can provide much-needed support during tough times.

4. Set Goals: They give you a sense of purpose and direction, making each setback less daunting.

7.4. Fostering Perseverance

Perseverance is the consistent effort to keep going despite difficulties, failures, or delays in achieving success. It's the fuel that keeps our desires and aspirations alive. Some methods to amplify your perseverance:

1. Start Small: Small steps can lead to big achievements. The aim here is to build momentum, not to conquer all at once.

2. Surround yourself with Positivity: Associating with positive influences shields you from negativity and discouragement.

3. Embrace Failures: Instead of seeing failures as the end, view them as learning experiences. Each failure brings you one step closer to success.

4. Stay Focused: Hold onto why you started in the first place. Your 'why' will keep you anchored when things get tough.

7.5. Resilience, Perseverance, and Self-Sabotage

By nurturing resilience and perseverance, we establish a safeguard against self-sabotage. Resilience equips us to handle setbacks and recover from them quicker. It ensures that a single failure or setback doesn't make us question our entire journey.

On the other hand, perseverance keeps us moving forward. It ensures that we don't give up at the first sign of trouble. It reminds us that most worthwhile goals require hard work, persistence, and time.

7.6. Strategies to Use Resilience and Perseverance Against Self-Sabotage

1. Practice Mindfulness: Being present allows us to identify self-sabotaging patterns early on. It creates space between stimulus and response, enabling us to react thoughtfully instead of impulsively.

2. Perform a Courage Audit: Jot down instances where you displayed courage and resilience. Reflecting on them can instill belief in your capabilities.

3. Adopt a Growth-Mindset: Encourage yourself to view challenges as opportunities to learn and grow.

4. Establish a Support System: Surround yourself with positive, uplifting individuals who can offer advice, motivation, and reassurance in times of need.

By developing resilience and perseverance, you're able to sidestep the pitfalls of self-sabotage. The road to self-improvement is not easy; it will test you, and there will be setbacks. However, with resilience and perseverance at your side, you're armed to face anything that comes your way. Remember, greatness isn't achieved overnight, it's a journey of continuous growth and self-discovery.

Hold onto these words by Theodore Roosevelt, "It is hard to fail, but it is worse never to have tried to succeed." So, dare to try, stumble, fall, rise, learn and keep moving forward! Embrace the power within you, the power of resilience and perseverance.

Chapter 8. Mastering Goal Management to Combat Self-defeating Behaviors

Human potential is limitless when unbridged by adverse mental constructs. Consider "self-sabotage", one of the dominant deterrents to achieving personal success, which often manifests in recurring patterns of self-defeating behaviors. It is crucial to diagnose, rewire, and replace these maladaptive patterns with actions that drive us toward our goals. This section meticulously dissects the techniques of mastering goal management, capable of countering self-destructive habits, and equips you with effective tools to navigate the journey of personal success.

8.1. Recognizing Self-Defeating Behaviors

Before anything, it is pivotal to recognize self-defeating behaviors, often epitomized by procrastination, perfectionism, fear of failure, and negative self-talk. These behaviors persist as they are insidiously tied to avoiding discomfort and seeking immediate gratification – irrespective of the long-term consequences. Accurate identification paves the way for initiating transformative changes.

8.2. Establish Clear Goals

The initial step to countering self-sabotage involves setting clear, measurable, and attainable goals. Grounded in the abundant literature on goal setting, SMART Goals - Specific, Measurable, Attainable, Relevant, and Time-Bound, serve as the primary tool. Be explicit about what you want to achieve (Specific), quantify or gauge progress tangibly (Measurable and Attainable), ensure alignment with broader objectives (Relevant), and finally, set a deadline to deliver added incentive (Time-Bound).

8.3. Breaking Down Goals into Manageable Tasks

One common trigger of self-defeating behaviors is feeling overwhelmed by the enormity of the goal. Overcoming this involves breaking down the goal into smaller, manageable tasks. Preparing a flowchart or roadmap, including all necessary subtasks and milestones, is a useful strategy. Celebrate every small victory along the way; this bolsters morale and maintains enthusiasm.

8.4. Modify Goal Unrealistic Expectations

Self-sabotage often stems from unrealistic expectations related to our abilities or the process of achieving our goals. This leads to inevitable lapses, culminating in disappointment, negativity, and cessation of efforts. Modulating expectations and accepting that success is rarely a straight road paves the way for healthier striving.

8.5. Build Resilience and Anticipate Setbacks

The journey towards personal success is fraught with numerous setbacks. Instead of cowering in the face of adversity, it is imperative to embrace the opportunity to learn from these setbacks. Developing resilience minimizes the adverse impact of hindrances, ensuring continuity in working towards our goals.

8.6. Prioritize and Manage Time Efficiently

Efficient time management is fundamental to goal achievement. Use tools such as the Eisenhower matrix to prioritize tasks based on urgency and importance. Regularly review and revise the schedule to adapt to unexpected changes or new obligations.

8.7. Instill/Sustain Motivation

Maintaining motivation is critical in goal management. Implement strategies such as visualization, positive affirmation, and self-reward systems. Recognizing and celebrating small victories keep morale high, thus minimizing the tendency for self-sabotage.

8.8. Maintaining Accountability

Being accountable amplifies commitment, thereby reducing the allure of adverse behaviors. Share your goals with supportive friends or family, use a mentor or coach, or try a digital tool to keep track of progress.

8.9. Effective Coping Strategies

Develop effective coping strategies to manage stress, anxiety, or feelings of overwhelm that usually trigger self-defeating behaviors. Practice mindfulness, employ relaxation techniques, or engage in regular physical activities.

8.10. Seek Professional Help

Lastly, if self-sabotage tendencies seem unmanageable, don't hesitate to seek professional help. Psychologists and life coaches provide targeted strategies, helping alter thought patterns and behaviors to optimize goal realization.

By using these techniques, you can successfully manage your goals, regardless of the challenges or obstacles you face. Remember, the journey is as important as the destination. By mastering goal management and combating self-defeating behaviors, you're well on your way to success. Enjoy the journey!

Chapter 9. Emotional Intelligence: The Key to Quieting the Inner Critic

Undeniably, each one of us has encountered our personal inner critic. It's that all too familiar voice inside our head that criticizes our every move, doubting our capabilities, undermining our efforts, and always ready to predict the worst-case scenarios. Your inner critic might echo remarks like, "I'm a failure," "I'm too dumb to learn this," or "I'm doomed to make the same mistakes again." However, by applying the principles and practices of Emotional Intelligence, we can learn to manage and quieten this critical inner voice.

9.1. Understanding Emotional Intelligence

Emotional Intelligence (EI) is the capacity to understand, manage, and effectively express one's own feelings, as well as engage and navigate successfully with those of others. Simply put, EI can be categorized into four types: self-awareness, self-management, social awareness, and relationship management.

1. **Self-awareness** involves recognizing and understanding your own emotions, strengths, weaknesses, values, and drivers. Being self-aware signifies understanding how your feelings and actions can affect those around you.

2. **Self-management** is about managing your feelings and impulses, and taking responsibility for your own performance. Individuals who are excellent in self-management often manifest integrity and tend to stay calm, clear, and focused during stressful situations.

3. **Social Awareness** implies understanding and attuning to others' emotional needs and concerns. It involves empathizing with others, understanding the power dynamics in a group or organization, and recognizing and meeting client needs.

4. **Relationship Management** is about managing and inspiring others, influencing them positively, communicating clearly, and demonstrating strong leadership skills.

9.2. How Emotional Intelligence Quiets the Inner Critic

By enhancing emotional intelligence, you can transform the way you perceive and approach your inner critic. Instead of seeing it as an enemy, you can view it as an informant that can provide you valuable insights about your deeper self. You can use the four components of emotional intelligence to combat self-sabotage effectively.

1. **Self-awareness**: Acknowledge the presence of your inner critic. Ignoring it only leads to further dissent. Bridge the gap between you and your critical voice. Recognize when it speaks and what triggers it. What situations or events evoke its harsh criticism?

2. **Self-management**: Learn how to soothe your critic rather than fighting it. Respond to the mind chatter with kindness. Reassure it by saying, "Thank you for your opinion, but I choose a different path."

3. **Social-Awareness**: Attune to the emotions of people around you. You pick cues on how to respond to situations by observing others responding in a similar context. Understand that everyone has an inner critic and watch how successful individuals handle theirs.

4. **Relationship Management**: Develop healthy relationships with others by helping them deal with their inner critic. Be a source of

positivity and encouragement. Your words can help others silence their critical voice, reinforcing your tactics against your critic.

9.3. Boosting Emotional Intelligence

Enhancing emotional intelligence isn't an overnight task. It requires practice, patience, and an open mind. Here are some strategies to boost your emotional intelligence:

1. Self-reflection: Practice mindfulness and meditation. Spend some time each day in quiet reflection, noticing your thoughts, feelings, and emotions without judgement.

2. Journaling: Writing down your thoughts can provide clarity. It's a safe space to express yourself freely, understand your triggers, and evaluate your emotions.

3. Active listening: Being a good listener is an essential aspect of emotional intelligence. Rather than focusing on your response, fully pay attention to other people when they're speaking, showing empathy and understanding.

4. Emotional regulation: Recognize the difference between responding and reacting. To respond is to choose how you act, whereas a reaction is led by raw emotion and can lead to regret.

5. Develop resilience: Resilience is the ability to bounce back from adversity. Enhance your resilience by focusing on your strengths, maintaining a positive attitude, and creating and carrying out realistic plans.

9.4. Overcoming the Pitfalls of the Inner Critic

It's empowering to realize and understand that we have the ability to manage our inner critics. Here are some practical steps to overcome the pitfalls:

1. Balance Negative with Positive: While your inner critic might focus on negatives, make sure you consciously focus on strengths and positive aspects too.

2. Talk back to your Critic: Confront your inner critic whenever it speaks. Have a positive counter-argument ready to rebut the criticism.

3. Replace Self-Criticism with Self-Supporting Statements: Swap negative statements like "I can't" with powerful, positive affirmations like, "I can handle whatever comes."

4. Practice Self-Compassion: Be kind to yourself. Work to create a warm, understanding relationship with yourself rather than indulging in criticism and judgment.

In conclusion, emotional intelligence is your key to quieten your inner critic. By harnessing the power of emotional intelligence, you can transform the way you perceive yourself and approach potential hurdles on your path to success. A heightened emotional intelligence allows for a balanced life, filled with self-compassion, resilience and positive affirmations, silencing the inner critic that often sabotages our strides to achievement.

Chapter 10. Practical Mindfulness Techniques for Daily Boost of Positivity

Mindfulness, a term you may have come across numerous times, is about being consciously present in the current moment - cognizant of your thoughts, feelings, sensations, and surroundings without judgment. Even though it sounds simple enough, practicing mindfulness can be challenging, especially amongst a fast-paced lifestyle. It requires dedication, patience, and practice. This part of the report includes practical mindfulness techniques designed to infuse daily bouts of positivity in your life.

10.1. Starting the Day Right

Remember the first few minutes after you wake up lay the foundation for your entire day. When achieving success becomes a priority, it's crucial to ensure these precious moments are tuned towards positivity.

- The first mindful hack of the day is to avoid jumping straight into the world of virtuality and social media as soon as you wake up. The barrage of news, messages, and social updates has the potential to overwhelm your senses and steer your morning towards stress.

- Start your day by engaging in a quick 5-minute mindfulness meditation, focusing on your breathing. Sit in a comfortable position, close your eyes, and start noticing your breath – its rhythm, depth, and the sensation it creates in your body. This exercise will gently nudge you into the present, setting a calm and positive tone for the day.

10.2. Mindful Eating

Food forms an essential part of our lives, yet we often overlook the process of consuming it. Mindful eating is about savoring each bite, bringing awareness to the flavors, texture, and aroma of the food, recognizing your feelings of hunger and satiety.

- Try to schedule at least one meal a day when you can practice mindful eating without multitasking. Eating without distractions, relishing the food, and being aware of its nutritional value can significantly enhance your relationship with food and overall well-being.

- During meals, make sure to chew your food properly and notice the influence of different ingredients on the overall flavor. Acknowledge the role food plays in nourishing your body.

10.3. Incorporating Active Meditation into Routine Tasks

You would be surprised at how routine tasks can transform into mindful meditations when performed with complete awareness.

- Everyday tasks such as washing dishes, taking a shower, or even brushing your hair can become a mindfulness technique if you fully engage in the sensory experience - notice the foamy soap, the water temperature, or the sensation of the brush on your scalp.

- Active meditation expands the scope of mindfulness to include all aspects of your life, not just the moments you dedicate to sitting meditation.

10.4. Stress Reduction through Mindful Breathing

Stress has the ability to cloud our judgment and muddle our thoughts. It's where mindful breathing techniques rise to the occasion, acting as a quick and available tool to restore tranquility and positive mindset.

- Whenever you find yourself dealing with intense emotions, take a pause, and focus on your breathing. Feel the inhalation and exhalation - the rise and fall of your abdomen along with your breath. Let this cycle of breath anchor you in the present, moving you away from stress and towards peace.

- Practicing regular "breath breaks" throughout the day can serve as mini resets for your mind, boosting positivity and productivity.

10.5. Mindful Walking for Enhanced Connectivity

Walking is another activity often performed on autopilot. However, when mastered, mindful walking can act as a powerful technique to reconnect with our bodies and surroundings.

- Whether you're walking from one room to another or taking a stroll outside, stay attuned to your movement - the rhythm of your steps, the sensation of your feet touching the ground, the slight sway of your body.

- Pairing this exercise with a gratitude practice amps up its positivity quotient. As you walk, silently express gratitude for various aspects of life such as the strength to walk, the beauty of nature around, or simply the gift of living.

10.6. Cultivating Positive Relationships through Mindful Listening

Building positive relationships is essential for personal success, and mindful listening could be the golden key. It's about fully engaging in a conversation, free from interjecting or constructing a response while the other person is talking.

- During conversations, maintain eye contact, and genuinely listen. Avoid distractions and remain present in the dialogue, showing respect and value to the speaker.

- Observe your internal reactions to the conversation without judgment. Keep an open mind, allowing new reflections, learning, and positive interpersonal connections to foster.

Our quick tour of practical mindfulness techniques for a daily positivity boost has ended, dear reader, but your journey is just commencing. Adopt these strategies, bring allegiance to present moments and watch your life fill with positivity, productivity, and potential. As famously said by Jon Kabat-Zinn, the founder of Mindfulness-Based Stress Reduction (MBSR), "You can't stop the waves, but you can learn to surf." Welcome aboard on this grand adventure of mindful surfing towards success.

Remember, whatever method you choose, what matters most is practice. Mindfulness skills develop through consistent practice. So start today, start now, and embark on this transformative journey to success.

Chapter 11. The Action Plan: From Self-Sabotage to Rock-Solid Self-Support

It's true that change can be challenging, but it's also a pathway leading to growth and advancement. As we shed light on the shadowy corners of our self-sabotaging habits, we equip ourselves with the tools to shape a future where we are our own biggest supporters. The transformation from undermining our potential to fortifying our resources involves cultivating healthier ways of thinking, learning to manage emotions, and building resilience towards setbacks. In this chapter, we bring all these dimensions together to construct a comprehensive plan of action.

11.1. Unmasking the Saboteur: Understanding Your Self-Sabotaging Patterns

The first step towards change is understanding. Start by identifying the patterns triggering your self-sabotaging tendencies. Do they stem from fear or anxiety? Are they fueled by an inner critic continually saying you aren't good enough? Or are these patterns rooted in a misguided desire for comfort that leads you to resist challenges?

Each person's self-sabotage is unique, formed from a complicated matrix of past experiences, beliefs, and internal narratives. So, take up a regular practice of self-reflection and introspection. Keep a journal or make mental notes over time. Confronting your self-sabotaging patterns isn't an excuse to beat yourself up. Instead, it's about acknowledging them as a part of your way of coping and providing a foundation of understanding upon which you can cultivate change.

11.2. Building a Toolbox: Strategies to Counter Self-Sabotage

1. **Mindfulness and Self-awareness**: Incorporate regular mindfulness practices in your schedule such as meditation, yoga or simple deep-breathing exercises. This enhances self-awareness, helping you identify triggering situations and address them proactively.

2. **Positive Affirmations**: Learn to rewire your negative thought patterns to positive ones using affirmations. Repeat phrases like "I am capable," "I am enough" or "I can overcome this" daily. Write them, speak them out loud, or meditate on them - each method works towards subduing that inner critic.

3. **Constructive Self-Talk**: Be mindful of how you converse with yourself. Replace harsh self-criticism with compassionate and constructive feedback.

4. **Healthy Coping Mechanisms**: Develop a range of strategies to handle stress, discomfort, and setbacks. This could be a physical activity, a calming hobby or speaking to a loved one about your feelings.

5. **Setting Realistic Goals**: Part of self-support is setting yourself up for success. That means setting achievable, clearly defined goals that allow for progress and avoid setting you up for failure.

11.3. Developing Resilience: The Supportive Power of a Growth Mindset

A 'growth mindset' embodies the belief that abilities and intelligence can develop with effort, learning, and persistence. It opposes the 'fixed mindset' which restricts individuals to the belief that their potentials are innate and unchangeable. Embrace the power of yet – where you may not be skilled 'yet', but will develop the capacity over time. This attitude fosters resilience, empowering you to view challenges as opportunities rather than impediments.

11.4. The Synergy of Mental and Physical Health

Caring for your physical health can have an incredible impact on your psychological well-being. Regular exercise, adequate sleep, and a balanced diet all contribute to better mental health. A healthy body leads to sharper cognitive functioning, stabilized mood, and improved stress response - essential guardrails against self-sabotage.

11.5. Cultivating Support: Building a Network

While this journey involves a great deal of self-reliance, it's also about recognizing the importance of external support. Accept assistance from mentors or loved ones, solicit feedback, and open up to their encouragement.

Remember that you aren't alone in this journey. Many others experience self-sabotage too, and by opening up about your struggle, you may help them feel less alone while fortifying your own resolve.

11.6. Committing to the Journey: Consistency and Patience

Lastly, recognize that the shift from self-sabotage to self-support isn't an overnight process, but a journey requiring consistency and patience. Keep iterating on your coping strategies, reflecting on your experiences, learning new tools and giving yourself grace when things aren't perfect. With persistence and courage, you can turn your internal narrative into one of empowerment and eventually arrive at a place of rock-solid self-support.